Ordinary Mourning

ABZ Series in Poetry

Ordinary Mourning

poems by

Carrie Shipers

ABZ

ABZ POETRY PRESS

First Edition 2010
Manufactured in the United States of America

All inquiries and permission requests should be addressed to the Editor, ABZ Press, PO Box 2746, Huntington WV 25727-2746.

Cover Painting by Laura Eklund

Cover Design by Lisa Bridges

CATALOGING DATA
Shipers, Carrie
Ordinary Mourning / Carrie Shipers. – 1st ed.
p. cm. – (ABZ First Book Poetry Series)
ISBN-13: 978-0-9801-560-2-7 (pbk. alk. paper)

Library of Congress Control Number: 2009910706

I. Title. II. Series

CONTENTS

SECTION THREE

FOREWORD

The amazing thing about *Ordinary Mourning* is that it sustains an obsessive focus on one subject – the relation between the dead and the living – without losing vitality. Carrie Shipers has contemplated the phenomenon – or illusion – of *haunting* from many more angles than you would have expected. The book takes on a kind of compulsively encyclopedic quality, so committed to its obsession that a reader's possible skepticism about ghosts and haunting will tend to dissolve along the way. Yet *Ordinary Mourning* as a whole does not insist that there is an afterlife, or that the spirits of the dead return to us as ghosts; what the book does assume is that the sensation of being visited, or haunted, by the dead is a common sensation, a feeling so "ordinary" (even if spooky!) as to be inseparable from being human. Not that ghosts demand your attention every day, but that if you have cared intensely about someone who has died, sooner or later a moment will come when you feel visited – or when you try desperately to feel so.

The longing to believe that the dead are not simply *gone* is the force that drives the voices in these poems, whether agonized by grief or more calmly baffled by silence like the speaker of "Caretaker":

I used to think
the newest dead would have the most to say,

but something keeps them from speaking.
Maybe they need time to understand where
they've gone, how long they'll have to stay.
I eat my lunch among wind-scoured stones,

inscriptions scraped clean, and sing old songs
I think they'll know. When I stop I hear
the silence louder than before. The dead
have less to say than I thought they would.

Depending on how you see it, many of the speakers in the book are much more sensitive to communications from the dead, or much more willing to be deluded. There is the miner's wife in "Commemoration" who lowers poisoned bread into a mineshaft intending to kill her husband's ghost because – since his death in a mine accident – his ghost has been driving her crazy. There is the fireman in "Peripheral Vision" who has seen so many terrible injuries that now he "sees" disastrous events happening everywhere. There is the 19th-century con-man photographer in "Spirit Photography" who has sold his customers photos in which their dead loved ones appear, and then finds his own wife's apparition in the shadows of a self-portrait he made not knowing that she had died the night before at her sister's house. There is the policeman in "Last Call" who believes that a woman named Suzy keeps phoning him, twenty years after she was murdered by her ex-husband; on the night of her death she did call the policeman asking for help. There is Sarah Winchester who has converted her house into an intricate maze in order to baffle the "spirits" who killed her family. There is the widow in "A Year and a Day" who calmly reports how long it took her to believe that her dead husband was entirely gone. There is the widower in "Double Vision" who has learned to see the dead but only unimportant ghosts, not the ghost of his wife. There is the woman in "After | Life" who wonders whether she herself has become a ghost.

That catalogue gives some idea of the range of characters in *Ordinary Mourning*, but there's much more. There are poems whose characters sadly or bitterly lament the *absence* of ghosts, and a few who are grateful for that absence. Meanwhile, in another current we hear from the dead themselves, who find their afterlife onerous, disappointing or dreary. The dead husband in "Failure to Appear" wants his wife to forget him and move on: "I'd give anything to keep from going back." The ghosts in "The Unseen Ghosts" are endlessly frustrated by their inability to have decisive impact on the living. The dead man in "Graveyard Shift" complains that his endless vigil in the cemetery feels unnecessary: "I thought I was going to my rest, / but I'm more tired than I ever was alive."

Amazingly resourceful in finding angles on its subject, *Ordinary Mourning* is also relentless in its commitment to the subject. Carrie Shipers decided to go all the way with it, running the risk that abundance would become redundancy. Fortunately she has enough power-of-language, and enough shrewdly strategic eerie elusiveness, to keep the reader curious about what her next angle will be. If a few of the poems remain a shade too puzzling, well, the arena where ghosts meet the living is a shady and puzzling place. *Ordinary Mourning* succeeds in making us feel we have explored that arena, with Shipers as our alarmingly cool guide. Rooted in the conviction that we will all sooner or later need a ghost or two, this is a book that won't be easily forgotten – perhaps a haunting book.

Mark Halliday

For Randal

During the Victorian era, mourning was divided into four distinct phases: full, second, ordinary, and half. During ordinary mourning, which typically lasted six months, women could wear black or black-and-white dresses of any fabric and could add black ribbon, lace, embroidery, or jet embellishments.

And to die is different from what anyone supposed, and luckier.

Walt Whitman

SECTION ONE

On the Nature of Belief

I know there's more to the world than what
we see, especially in a world where no one
sees enough. Yet even on a vampire tour

of New Orleans after two bloody marys
left my tongue and forehead burning,
vodka was the only spirit I could name.

I've never seen a single ghost, no women
swathed in black, men wronged by love
or anger. At home, I jerk my head

at unfamiliar shadows or shafts of light,
sounds I think I hear, but it's always nothing—
a crooked window blind, my upstairs neighbor

dropping her shoes. I want a ghost to call
my own, one willing to visit every night,
who looks enough like me I won't be startled.

Open House

When I found his body, I wanted to flee,
wanted to lock the doors and hold him
until I starved. A week after the funeral,
the neighbors' wives offered to help me pack.
For where? I asked. *Suicides are restless*,
they hissed as I walked them to the door.

Every house in town has had its deaths:
emphysema, heart attacks, teenagers airborne
through a barbed wire fence. And that's not counting
the ones no one remembers: children taken
by measles or morbid sore throat, women dead
of childbirth or despair, patriarchs expiring
in the family bed. Two hundred years ago,
I could have wept and torn my hair, worn only black,
opened his grave and embraced his corpse.
I sent his suits to Goodwill, sold his car.

At night, grief sits on his half of the sofa.
It follows me upstairs. I know what I hear:
the house settling on its foundation, raccoons
rummaging the attic, wind sweeping trees.
I'll take him back in any form he chooses—
a loose brick above the fireplace, steam
streaking the bathroom mirror, a window
gaping when it rains. I'd give anything
to see his ghost. It's only grief that haunts me.

Living Among the Dead

I expected mist or fog drifting, not this hard
Hopper light, a sun I can't see shining
on and through. I'd imagined the dead
living in houses, or something like houses,
imagined them having lives—loved ones,
laughter, meals to prepare. Across the plain
I saw a high school classmate who was killed
by a grain auger. I called his name.
He turned, waved, walked on. I watched
his legs scissor the ground's slow unfurling,
wondering if he'd forgotten me,
if I'd forgotten some teenage grudge
he'd died holding. When I caught up to him,
I asked how he was. *All right, I guess.*
The weather's a little dry. He nodded
toward what might have been the horizon.
Have you seen your dad? I asked. *Not yet.*
I heard he's here somewhere. If the dead
have ghosts, it must be the living
who haunt them. A murdered woman called me
by her husband's name. *I'm not the man*
who killed you, I said as gently as I could.
I know, she said. If the dead hunger,
it isn't for revenge. Like them,
I have no need to eat, though I'd like
to feel bread tearing between my teeth,
blueberries snapping open on my tongue.
My hands hang useless on their hinges.
There's little here that can stand our touch.

Resurrection

Sago, 2006

I know folks wish I'd died. I'd like to meet
with the families, but I'm still confused.

I'm afraid I'll use the wrong names,
give one man the joke or lunchbucket

that belonged to another. Underground,
you hear rock and water but also stories—

picks at work in machine-dug shafts,
headlamps where none could be. The lights

in our helmets flicker before they go out,
as, the preacher says, do we.

I imagine people in Bethany wondered
why Lazarus deserved a miracle

their dead didn't, the same question he asked
each night, afraid if he closed his eyes

he'd wake in the grave again, or not at all.
I didn't ask to live any louder or harder

than the ones who walked that last tunnel
into light as clean as sunrise.

I figure they'll forgive me when they can.

Overtime

I'll rest when I'm dead, my father says. Salt stains
his overall straps, his hammer's rubber handle.
I know he thinks it's true, but I've seen him,
laid off by brutal winter or wet spring, polish
lawnmower engines piece-by-piece or rearrange
my mother's kitchen. He taught me work could cure
the worst in us—outlast anger, soothe sorrow's
keening ache. If he haunts me, I'll know
by what he does: ice scraped from my windshield,
a bookcase steadied while I sleep. I imagine him
muddy to his knees, eating lunch—*dinner*, he says—
in a diner filled with men who won't stop working:
truckers with phantom rigs; miners of closed shafts;
farmers who plow the fields in which they died;
men whose lives are marked by what they've made.
I hope, when he dies, he keeps the life he loves.
Without his work, I wouldn't know who he was.

Caretaker

I like it best when I'm alone—no children
climbing the stones, no mourners marking loss
with tears or twisted wreaths. The din of burials
doesn't belong—sermons and weeping,

then the backhoe's growl. I can't hear
till the chairs and tarps are folded, the new grave
the same as the others. I used to think
the newest dead would have the most to say,

but something keeps them from speaking.
Maybe they need time to understand where
they've gone, how long they'll have to stay.
I eat my lunch among wind-scoured stones,

inscriptions scraped clean, and sing old songs
I think they'll know. When I stop I hear
the silence louder than before. The dead
have less to say than I thought they would.

Patrolling

My first night solo, a Buick flagged me down
at 3 am: man, wife, two boys in the back seat.
He said he'd stopped to rest, then couldn't get
the car restarted. I turned my back to call
for help, heard the car start up and drive away.
I told the story after shift, drinking coffee
when I should've showered and gone home.
He killed them all, Sarge said when I finished.
Last night? I couldn't believe I'd let him go.
About ten years back, I think.

Two months later
I was writing up a crash—four girls in a red
Beretta with specialty plates—when she knocked
on my window. *Are my friends okay?* Two blocks
from the hospital, she disappeared. Sarge called me in
on my day off. *That girl was already dead.*
Your dispatcher thinks you're too crazy to wear
a badge, let alone a gun. He narrowed his eyes.
Help them if you can, but for chrissakes
keep it off the radio.

If people looked, they'd see
the plates on my cruiser are expired, my uniform
out of date. I haven't worked for the state
since a semi hit me on Highway 5. No one saw
why I stopped, the station wagon on its roof,
driver who looked like my wife. My job's the same
as always: I help the ones I can, and the ones
I can't seem comforted by the uniform,
the knowledge someone will witness their deaths.

Visitation

My mother waited years
to tell me: the morning after
my high school graduation,

she found her dead stepfather
eating chocolate cake in the living room.
She said, *Good morning.*

He nodded and licked blue frosting
from a plastic fork. She knew
she was awake. She could hear

the refrigerator's solemn hum,
birds outside at the feeder.
She wondered how he'd found

his way to a house built five years
after his death, wondered why
her mother hadn't come—

but the dead deserve their rest.
She drank a glass of water
and went back to bed.

When she got up again,
the evidence—fork, plate, crumbs—
could've belonged to anyone.

Homestead

Everywhere I look, I see what I've done wrong:
the soddy's crooked corners, two cattle dead
of larkspur, the scar on my right arm. Before
we left Ohio, she said she needed trees the way
I needed sky, needed to spit without looking
over my shoulder. I promised her a house—
two stories, a chimney made of stone—
once we had money for wood. At the end
of our first winter, I brought her thread and ribbon,
the candy she loved when we were courting.
I brought the axe inside to hone. Outside,
the April snow I'd raced from town. When she said
she wanted to leave, I swung without thinking
how close the walls had gotten since October.
The ground is as hard to dig as it is to plow.
I evened the corners as best I could, put aside
the rocks my shovel struck. I should have gone
to town and told my story, but spring came
overnight. It was time to plant our fields. She sits
on the unmade bed or rocks in the willow chair
I made. Her wheat-green eyes see everything:
my work-clothes crusted in a corner, the black-
bottomed cornbread I eat at every meal.
Out here, we have to live with our mistakes.

Commemoration

Husband, I've brought the bread
you asked for and a length of twine
to lower into the mine's waiting mouth.
Between its edges, there's barely room
for your voice. It might be wind,
my own bloody pulse. All morning
our children cried with hunger.
Tomorrow I'll use the last oats for porridge
and have nothing I can bring you.
The men you ask after are all dead.
You are blocking the way to their bodies.

Women hiss at me in the store, the street:
Widow, wear black. Clear your kitchen table
for the body our men will bring. I miss
your blue-freckled skin. Without
your furnace-body, I shake and shiver
in a bed stained gray with what
you can't wash off. The children sleep
with fists against their tender bellies.

I've heard the story they teach in church,
the miner's wife who celebrated mass
for her missing husband—a loaf of bread,
a jug of wine, a candle. Jealous, the devil
came to whisper, *Your husband's dead.*
Save what you have. For three days the wife
stayed home. On the fourth, she ignored
the devil and returned to church.
The miner, rescued after many days,
said he'd had food and wine for all but three.

Husband, you must eat the bread
I've brought you. Tear its crust with your
soot-fingers, grind it between coal-teeth.
I begged the poison from our priest.
I said the rats wouldn't let me rest,
that they bit the children, stole our food.
Husband, I've decided to save what I can.

Lucy Bell Speaks

Beginning in 1817, the Bell family of Adams, Tennessee, was plagued by a series of mysterious occurrences, most of which centered on the youngest daughter, Betsy. Although many events attributed to "The Bell Witch" are well-documented, no credible explanation has ever been found.

I didn't want John to die. His affliction
was enough—tongue swollen, face twitching
so hard he couldn't speak or swallow.
I was twelve when he bought me from my father.
He didn't know my mother was a witch
or what I'd learned. At first I thought I'd failed,
that the rocks falling on the roof, crashes
that called us from our beds, were only pranks.
Sweet Betsy, with her wheat-gold hair
and astonished eyes, was no more a child
than I had been. I saw how her father looked
at her, how often the schoolteacher kept her late
for lessons, boys trailing her like vines.
The spirit left welts with its slapping, bruises
when it threw her to the floor, but I tried
to keep her safe. Every night, men came
to find out what the spirit knew. I learned the Bible
at my father's knee and then John Bell's.
It matched them verse for verse.

I told John
the spirit would let us be if Betsy married.
I don't think she wanted what he did,
but she never said a word to stop it. I loved them both
too much to choose, do more than I already had.

When the doctor touched my husband's lips
and whispered *Poison*, my daughter's hands
were stained with nightshade berries.
Like John, the spirit chose her over me.

Peripheral Vision

Don't look directly at the dead, they said
when I worked my first disaster, a fire that scorched
the heart of town. I study wounds instead
of faces, see hands move without thinking
what they do. I'm never ready for my shift
to end. Without spinning lights and sirens,
I have too much time to think about what
I see, what to do if what I see is real:
a woman folded across her steering wheel;
man brushing smoke from chest and throat;
child biting her sister's knee. Turning my head
so hard it hurts, I see each scene resolve:
she retrieves her cell phone; he throws down
his cigarette; the child says, *I kissed it*
so it wouldn't hurt.

My wife doesn't know
how often I stand beside our bed, see blood
cooling on the quilt, her broken skull. I used to slide
my hands over the blanket, testing each limb
for tenderness or dislocation—until the night
she woke up screaming. I've learned it's best
if I keep walking down the hall, the street.

Surrogate Ghost

After an April 26 auto accident, a family sat by the bedside of a woman they believed to be their daughter for weeks before realizing that she was instead another college student injured in the wreck.

Associated Press, 6/1/06

I remember grabbing her hand when the van
rolled over, wrist snapping inside my sleeve
as she flung forward. My picture on the lid

of the casket, my parents' bowed heads. *Look,*
she said, *they're getting used to life without you.*
I try to understand how much her family

loved her, why they needed weeks to see
what I was too weak to say. After her parents
realized what they'd lost, after they moved her body

to a grave with her name instead of mine, I hope
she understood why I wouldn't take her place.
I never know which one of us to mourn.

Graveyard Shift

I don't remember my death, only my mind
snapping open when my casket touched earth.
My wife's hair shone in wheat-colored light.
She wore the navy blue dress she'd bought
for her sister's wedding. The last person buried
stands guard till the next one comes.
Before me, it was a little girl who'd drowned
in the family pond. *She liked peach pie*,
my wife said when we heard. *I should make one*
for her mother. I don't know if she did.
It's easier for children. They still remember
where they came from, don't mind the light
going back. My wife's remarried now.
I doubt she'll fill the space beside me.

There's nothing here I need to protect.
Sometimes teenagers chase each other
along the gravel paths or dare someone
to lay on a grave and close his eyes. Then one
reads a name he recognizes—a grandparent,
great-aunt, crazy third cousin he never knew—
and they walk to their cars and drive away.
There used to be more visitors—old ladies
with plastic flowers or trowels and real ones,
men who left their fields to cry tears
sharp as gravel. My wife came on Fridays.
I tried not to mind when she stopped.

No one here is a ghost, exactly, or if they were
they've given up. *It gets to be more trouble*
than it's worth, a woman told me. *To make them*

remember you, you have to remember them so hard
you can't do anything else. They've been
bad years for farming, the twenty I've been gone,
but the town must be gathering its dead
somewhere new. I thought I was going to my rest,
but I'm more tired than I ever was alive.

SECTION TWO

Living With the Dead

When a door drafts open, you must welcome
what wants in. Mine arrive just after dinner,
traveling in packs like teenagers. I whisper

Come in while I wash dishes, *Hello*
from the living room sofa. I've looked
for signs—symbols chalked on the doorstep,

suspicious arrangements of driveway gravel—
announcing my house as a meeting place,
but found nothing. Upstairs, I lay awake

listening to floorboards' jagged laughter,
the occasional moan of a door. I thought
the dead would be used to the quiet dark,

grateful to be warm, but they leave the lights
and radio burning, windows open to the cold.
I left a note: *Please put the furniture back*

where you found it. My broken mirror,
bloody footprints pointing to the stairs. If I moved,
I know they'd follow, trailing me like mist.

Spirit Photography

In 1861 [William Mumler] took a self-portrait and, after developing the photographic plate, noticed what appeared to be the image of a dead person next to his . . . . Individuals sat for photographers in hopes of seeing the faces of dead loved ones revealed in the print.

<u>*The Encyclopedia of Ghosts and Spirits*</u>

They pose as still as corpses, hoping to see
what they should feel. The camera records
without making choices: a patriarch's grave
expression, widow's torn glove. Later,
I add what the camera can't see: his wife
in bridal white; her soldier husband;
children in christening gowns or nightshirts.
I understand the need for proof, how sorrow
overrules suspicion. One night I locked the shop,
posed with the evidence of my success—
my name in gold script on the window,
the brocade backdrops, my best gray suit.
In the darkroom, faces crowded the frame:
mother, grandfather, maiden aunt sucking
her dentures—and my wife, who was living
with her sister in Indiana. In the morning,
I wrote: *I realize more than ever how brief*
our time may be. Let us waste no more apart.
I didn't mention the rigged plate, her face
among my dead. Her sister replied—a sudden fever,
my wife's passing the evening before I wrote.

If my work isn't real, someone had to make
my wife appear. I've asked every man
in my shop, even some of my rivals,
but no one will confess. Each night
I try again—the suit I would've worn
to her funeral, black drapes to signify grief,
her mourning ring on my smallest finger.

Double Vision

When I saw the ad, *Learning to See the Dead,*
I expected a circle of folding chairs, people
who insisted the dead are alive in our hearts.
Instead, I learned how light leaves them
differently than it does us, leaves shadows
of lavender or sage, bruises that look like grief.
I see strangers, mostly, or people I didn't know
had died: my third grade teacher, college
classmates, the man who delivered my mail.
Carrying purses and briefcases, the dead move
with at least as much purpose as we do. They say
Hello or *Excuse me* or *How 'bout those Cards?*
The dead like baseball best, I suspect because
of the grass, the long stretches where nothing
seems to happen. If I mention my wife,
they pat my arm—the dead have clumsy hands—
and say she knows how to find me. When I die,
I wonder if I'll see more of them or fewer,
if I'll see myself as clearly as I see them.

Maggie Fox Speaks

In March 1848, Maggie Fox and her younger sister Kate were visited by the spirit of a murdered peddler buried in the cellar of their childhood home. The Hydesville rappings, as the incidents became known, marked the beginning of the Spiritualist movement that swept nineteenth-century America.

The rapping started as a prank to frighten Mother,
make Father doubt the God he drank like whiskey.
Poor white-faced Kate cried and clung
when the neighbors came, but we laughed
about it after. People traveled miles to hear
the Hydesville rappings, see the girls who spoke
to spirits. We couldn't stop it when we tried.
The spirits are angry, we said. *They'll speak to us*
no more. But when our friends rented a hall
in Rochester, the spirits said what to charge
and chose our gowns. I knew we were smarter
than the men who locked the doors and held
our hands and feet. They bound us to our chairs,
demanded we summon spirits, appointed their wives
to strip us and inspect our limbs.

By train
or hired carriage, we went where we were asked.
The little we made was spent on boarding houses,
hotels, doctors for Kate. The first time
the spirits made a table move I thought
she'd faint. I never told her what I'd planned—
she looked so pretty when she cried and wrung
her fingers sometimes even I believed.

Kate forgot, the years we worked apart—
none of it was real. When her husband died
she drank, our act too out-of-date to feed
her children. Other women spoke in trance
or—bound, gagged, and locked in a cabinet—
produced whole ghosts or gobs of spirit matter.
Maggie, she wrote, *the spirits are gone.*
Tell me what I've done. I refused to remind her
of the girls we'd been, bored by farmwork
and ignored by Father.

If what we did
was wrong, we didn't do it by ourselves.
It's lonely here. I've looked for Kate,
but don't know where or who she is.
We never imagined the dead like this.

Perpetual Care

We laid her in the ground last month. She'd asked
to be ashes, but I wanted a place I could go.
Our friends promise on the other side of this
wild grief lies peace. *For both of us*, I think.
They've taken my rifle and all her pills.
Her headstone hasn't come, only the brass plate
from the county with her name and dates.
Sun shines so hard the metal burns my hands.
The florist keeps my wife's daisies in the front
of the cooler. If he's busy, I reach for them
myself, breath held against their sweetness.

Next month or the one after, I'll work
past dark, go home to the television's comfort.
Weeks will pass before I notice how long
I've stayed away, and even though I'll think of her—
the scar on her left knee, smell of her neck
when she slept—visiting on her birthday
or our anniversary will feel, tucked between
the gym and grocery, like one more errand.
I mourn my wife, the grief I know won't last.

Reparation

Two miners whose jobs included watching for safety hazards inside the Sago Mine before the deadly explosion in January committed suicide in the past month.

Associated Press, 9/27/06

The papers will say I killed myself out of guilt
or fear, that I knew more about the explosion

than I let on. I told the state boys everything
I could. I knew one day I'd tell a judge—

in this world, or the other. Before my daddy died,
he warned me not to be an inspector. He'd seen

picket lines and scabs, the accidents both sides
staged. He said he knew the mine had ghosts,

but slept easier knowing they weren't his fault.
I don't have to go underground to see the men

who died. When I drive downtown, they stand
on the sidewalks and watch me pass. They crowd

the diner, the store, the line behind me at the bank.
The state said they weren't pressing charges,

but they aren't who I failed. When the strikes
got ugly, Daddy carried a gun in his lunch pail.

After all that damp, it still fires. Most folks
won't understand I have to do what's right,

but everywhere I go, I see twelve who will.
Some things a man's not meant to survive.

Last Call

As soon as I pick up, I know who and where
she is. I hear her breath catch as she whispers
Help, hear the bartender call *Last round*,
the shuffle of keys and beer-heavy feet. *Suzy*,
I say, *you know there's nothing we can do.*
My shift is three-quarters over. *He has a gun*,
she says. I switch the phone to the other ear.
You need to go home. She sighs so hard it hurts
my chest. Weekends there's a real emergency—
a housefire or flipped semi, maybe a shooting—
she doesn't call and I don't miss her.

Twenty years ago, there wasn't 911,
just a number the sheriff sometimes answered.
Suzy said her ex was waiting outside,
but the cruiser never came. Now I'm the one
she asks for help, though I always tell her no.
I think she calls because she knows I have
to answer, that she hopes, if not for help,
for sympathy, which I can't afford to give.

Spirit Winter

We were less afraid of the spirit than what
it knew. Its rapping rattled window glass,
jolted beds. No one slept. The first time
the mother cried, *What do you want with us?*
there was no answer till she and the spirit
agreed on terms—two raps for *yes*, none for *no*.
Like a schoolboy, the spirit spelled demands,
our preacher calling *A. . . B. . . C . . .* in the voice
that called us to our knees. He said the devil
was at work only if we believed it so, but what
could the devil want with folk like us?

The spirit knew our names, where we were born,
whose taxes were paid or overdue. It knew
us better than our neighbors did: Jeb Tyler's son
belonged to his brother, Beth Parker died
of suicide and not the fever that took her man.
We should have laid that thing to rest and let it be,
but it was winter, the mills and farms as still
as the dead should be. The night the preacher
stayed home sick, men called questions so fast
the spirit's answers pounded like a hammer.
My husband came home with blood on his knuckles
and shirt. He wouldn't speak and slept all day.
After supper, I climbed into the wagon.

The house was dark, and no one answered our shouts
and pounding. On the porch, a man raised an axe
but didn't swing. Another lit a torch, let it drop
in the snow. We stood all night in the cold,
chewing bits of news the spirit taught us,

then left at dawn to tend our stock. At breakfast
my husband spoke. *Tell me it isn't true*, he said.
That you married me because I was the only man
who asked, that you begged your father not to make
you go. My fingers crossed under my apron.
I married you for love.

No place to linger
even in the light, the spirit's house stands empty.
No one knows where the family went or if they took
the spirit with them. Felled by fever or God,
the preacher was dead by spring, and the town
nearly tore itself apart. It was work that saved us.
Planting came, and we were too tired to talk
about more than the weather, the acres left to plow.
When we met in church or town, we were tender
with each other, as tender as my husband's
callused hands when he turned to me again.

Playing Dead

Life was hard on the farms, my mother said
when I asked why Violet's stone didn't have dates
or *Beloved. Sometimes it was best to move on.*

At first Violet wouldn't set one foot outside
the cemetery gates. She said she wasn't afraid,
but when I went home for supper, she screamed
and pulled her hair: *You love your parents*

more than me. My mother thinks I stopped playing
with Violet when I fell in love with our neighbor's
teenage son. I never told her the truth: one day

she walked with me a step or two beyond
the gates. A week later, as far as the drainage ditch.
I was afraid she'd follow me farther, saw her
teasing my brothers, my mother brushing her hair.

On my last visit, I didn't say a word as I poured
a ring of salt around her flat white stone—
I knew she couldn't come unless I called.

The Logic of Grief

After the funeral, I sat all night on the porch.
A year ago, we watched the high school burn.
Broken windows, gasoline, two blank-faced boys
my husband taught. The firemen tried to save
the gym, but forgot the walled-up balcony stuffed
with stage curtains, textbooks too old to use,
too good to throw away. It took months
to understand what we'd lost: trophies won
by the town's grandfathers, sixty years
of class composites and permanent records.

We knew we couldn't keep the town alive
without our school. The principal put trailers
where the rubble had been, but basketball season
was disappointing, every game *Away* no matter what
the scoreboard said. Grief moves, like fire,
with a logic all its own, fingering what we think
is out of reach, ignoring our dry tinder. In June,
they took away the trailers, redrew the district lines.
In July, my husband put a gun to his head.
Under my skin, grief waits to see what burns.

Hank Williams, holy Father,

your howling scales my screen door
like a cat. I spike the floor
with bowls of milk and bourbon,
listen for claws clicking linoleum.
Instead: your locomotive cough,

steel guitar swallow. Fingers fret
my hollow spaces, tender planes
of skull and hip. How I long
to descend your banjo valley,
plumb your tambourine lake.

Snow climbed the hubcaps
of a rented Cadillac. You huddled
under coats piled between
open windows, waxy skin so hot
no one noticed you were gone.

Thumbs press fever into my forehead,
under my eyes. The radio

plays pieces of what we know.

Hank Williams, holy Father,
how I long to burn both with and for.

The Amateur Resurrectionist

He'd been dead six months. Mouthing the Latin
she'd learned to wake him, she threw herself
against his stone until she bruised, then lifted
her shovel and sank its blade. He emerged grave-
smeared and grateful, spine crackling behind
the split back of his jacket. He didn't ask
about the funeral—who came or how many
flowers, even how he'd died.

Together
they filled the hole, replaced its flap of sod.
She asked what being dead was like. *It's not
like anything.* She'd thought he could cure
her grief, but she felt it lodged low in her back,
one more thing, like restaurants and snow,
they couldn't share. In the dark, she dragged
his hands against her body, but his skin
was gray and cold. She couldn't sleep.

She told him everything—how much it hurt
to live with only part of him, how that first knot
of sorrow had climbed her spine and spread.
You aren't keeping me alive, he said,
just around. She buried him again,
each clot of dirt grief's fist unclenching.

After | Life

I stayed in the shower as long as I could,
then posed before the steam-shot mirror,
trying to remember what Frost said
about ghosts: if the dead *are* souls,
surely they don't have them? I've read
arguments about whether ghosts exist,
but none that tell if you are one.
I know a dozen times I could have died—
the fever that spiked in my sleep, a crash
two lanes away, the alley I avoided.
The people I see in the grocery and the park
don't seem dead. I might be haunting them,
though they look frightened only by their lives'
ordinary burdens. I feel different than I did
last night—lonelier and less afraid.
If that was life, this morning must be after.

Failure to Appear

I see her look under the bed, behind doors,
shove open the shower curtain. Her laugh
is sharper than I remembered, her shoulders
not as straight. She should move away
from the life we made, the house that held
my body. If I haunted her, I'd have
to stay behind, linger in a world I was glad
to leave. I'd have to rely on the living—
to see and hear me, to give me what I need.
Each day, a thousand small decisions—
what to eat or wear, how much to love—
my wife could forget me if she tried.
I'd give anything to keep from going back.

Vanishing Hitchhiker

I'm standing by the road in October
wearing nothing white. Your foot
presses the brake. The radio blinks static,
switches to a station you don't know.
This is the haunting you thought
you wanted. If you don't stop,
I'll follow you, heels striking sparks
on the center line. I'll hunker low
in your back seat.

Driving faster
at every bridge, what you feel
might be fear, but you don't stop
talking for miles, telling me nothing
I don't already know. You don't ask
my name, where I'm from or going to.
When I ask to be let out, you coast
to the shoulder, shadows of fence-posts
and scrub-oak, the loss that begins
when my door clicks closed.

You'll arrive home unharmed, surprisingly
hungry. You'll wish we'd shared
a kiss, or at least a question,
to make your version different
and more true. Already you know
no one will believe you, that each telling
will make it harder to believe
yourself. Your doors are locked,
keys waiting on the table.

SECTION THREE

State Route Y

What I thought I saw: a man walking
the gravel shoulder of a road I didn't know.
I pressed hard on the brake. He disappeared.
I drove faster around a curve, past a cemetery
that predated the highway, thirty stones
behind four feet of weedy chainlink.
It was the shadow of a mailbox, I told myself.
A smear on the windshield. They say
if you drive too long you see things.

I should've stopped, asked who he was
and what he wanted, why he'd chosen me.
Instead, I made excuses: too far south
to be a ghost of mine, he might've been
a man with car trouble or bad intentions.
If I'd stopped, I would've been in danger,
a dark two-lane no place for curiosity
or the semi that followed me for miles.
What haunts me most: my failure to believe.

Missing Four Months

The police took her toothbrush, address book,
the sheets from our bed, my fingerprints and picture.
Her purse and car—no keys or signs of struggle—

were discovered in a parking lot downtown.
She may have known her attacker. She may not
have been attacked. *Maybe*, the detective said,

she wanted somewhere warm, a man who isn't you.
He told me to change our locks. I lie awake
listening for her key. I don't care where she is

or why she left—if she calls, I'll come for her,
wire money anywhere she wants. If I see
her ghost, I'll know I'm not why she left.

Perlerorneq

Jim didn't know how to keep still.
Even when he slept, I could hear his breath
squeak in his lungs, his fingers grip
the bedclothes. Four days ago,
we went out into the white
to remind ourselves the world exists
with or without us. Jim's sealskin coat
is warmer than mine but his boots
are too damn small. Toes curl
against my soles. Cold shards
my bones. Without Jim, I can't be sure
I'm speaking out loud, if what I see
is the same as what he would.

Each day, I write a little of what
I've learned: the sound snow makes
before it falls, how we walked for days
without seeing anything alive,
the butt of my rifle splintering
against Jim's skull. His gun fell so far
into the snow I couldn't find it.
Without a way to hunt, I doubt I'll last
the winter. Dark settles on my chest
like a blanket, then a stone. Jim circles
the cabin without leaving a sign.
Like me, he wants to be warm.

Sarah Winchester Speaks

In 1884, rifle heir Sarah Winchester bought a six-room farmhouse in California and began renovations designed to trap the vengeful spirits she believed responsible for the deaths of her husband and daughter. When she died in 1922, the Winchester Mystery House contained more than 160 rooms and 40 staircases.

No one knew what haunted me:
soldiers bivouacking in the unfinished ballroom,
deer and buffalo stampeding parquet halls,
and every night my baby crying, always
from a different room. Choking on sawdust
and plaster, I drew stairs that stopped
at the ceiling, doors that opened
to blank walls or two-story drops, hallways
that doubled back. I gave my ghosts the best
of everything—Tiffany windows,
gold dinner service, thirteen-bulb chandeliers—
but couldn't put a single soul to rest
or rest myself. I died before I understood:
I haunted my house as much as they did.
William and the baby are waiting for me,
but I'm trapped by blind chimneys, skylights
stacked on top of each other, stairs I can't help
but climb, the maze I made to stay the dead.

The Unseen Ghosts

Too shy or embarrassed to make themselves known,
they open doors without a sound, move vases

and frames a fraction off-center. Fretting no less
than before, they wring intangible fingers.

Life after death is not what they expected.
They thought they'd have more courage, the power

to disrupt our crowded world. They thought
we'd pay more attention, be easier to anger

or dismay. Envious of those who are seen,
who bring comfort or demands, their hearts beat

behind invisible ribs: *I am nothing but rage,*
broken windows, whole sets of china smashed

into walls. What I can't touch I want to destroy—
chairs, peaches, your bitter skin. All my life, I saved

what I didn't say, let bile leach into my bones.
I say your name when the shower runs. You reach

for a towel. Your body moves through mine.
You barely shiver. They never lose their faith in us,

their belief that what we fail to see is not our fault.
They forgive far more than they should.

Living Without the Dead

I like the life I've made—no one to ask
how warm to sleep or what to eat, no one

watching television when I want to read.
I know how demanding the dead can be,

how greedy for revenge or attention.
I'm tired of steam rising from my cup,

rain lit by streetlights, my frosted breath,
tired of groaning stairs, stray kittens crying

on the porch. I like to hear my heart's
hard beating, air moving through my lungs,

see dust motes spinning in the light.
I've waited all my life to live alone.

Ghosting Around

Lilah's lipstick looked like blood. I used
Wisconsin Rose, the shade my mother wore.
The lobby looks like shit, she said the night
we met. *They need to paint the pillars*—
two flaking columns as slim as we were.
Unless we found a man to pay, Lilah and I
didn't eat. We carried, on our dates, daytime purses
big enough to hold entire loaves of bread,
baked potatoes, chicken or fish we wrapped
in napkins. At first, I waited tables for men
who smelled like work, then sold cosmetics
to women who looked right through me.
Lilah's pajamas were silk. *Men*, she'd sigh,
ice clicking her glass. After she left,
I'd wash lipstick off its rim and go to bed.

Snow followed me into the lobby.
I was thinking what a jerk my date had been,
how Lilah'd laugh and call me *sister*—
then saw her posed between the pillars, lipstick
staining her mouth. I kicked off my pumps,
ran like the farm girl I'd been. The landlord
said Lilah left Des Moines in a borrowed dress,
worked as a typist until her boss—*the jealous type*
with a service pistol—caught her stepping out.
How long ago? I asked. *About five years.*
She must like you if she wanted you to know.

Chicago's not the same—I knew it couldn't be.
Last spring, I went to see our building.
It was smaller than I remembered, the lobby
not as grand. White against white walls,
impossibly thin, the pillars looked like ghosts.
I stood between them and saw her kiss,
a perfect red bow. I pressed my lips to hers.

Highway Crosses

Knocked down by wind or careless mowers,
most don't survive the summer. Others bloom
balloons or plastic flowers, attempts to distinguish
one tragedy from another, a baby crushed
in a car seat, a trucker lucky he only killed
himself. They make me think of ghosts,
though I've never seen one, only miles
of tar-patched pavement, grass and weeds,
each square of shoulder the same as the next.

Inventory

The dead I keep: a woman burned as a witch
in nineteenth-century Ireland; a miner carrying
lunchbucket and shovel; two country-western stars;
one toothpaste suicide; a racecar driver clutching
his helmet; a train robber whose corpse appeared
in a sideshow. My most recent acquisitions:
an Iowa farmer dead in his sleep and the wife
who likely killed him.

Like any collector,
I'm guilty of greed and shortsightedness.
I've traded dead I should've kept, hoarded those
for whom I have no use. I used to believe
my dead chose me, but I've found myself cruising
newspaper morgues and coroners' reports,
perusing monographs with murderous titles.
The dead I know I mostly ignore, uncertain how
to interpret their deaths, what degree of affection
or proximity entitles me to grief. I prefer
to mourn the dead whose deaths I understand.

Housekeeping

I love this house for what's been left: dishrag
dried to the table, books and rubber boots
in the mud-room, a blue silk dress.

In the hour of afternoon she called her own,
she laid it against her sun-rough arms, waltzed
across the bedroom. I imagine what she saw:

work shirts crowding the clothesline; lilacs
blooming by the door; the husband who ate
the burnt potatoes, soggy chops she cooked

their whole first year. I fit my clothes inside
her drawers, radio on the shelf above her sink,
canned soup in the pantry beside her preserves.

If she comes, I'll say, *You were right to leave*
the front room curtains. Your husband took care
of his tools. She left more space than I can fill.

Living For the Dead

My husband loved our sons too much to let them
suffer a divorce. If he'd been strong enough
to follow through—the children, me, himself—
we would've stayed a family. After the funeral,
I carried their toys to the living room and stayed
awake all night. They never came.

Already
people are impatient with me and my grief.
They need me to prove they, too, could survive
the worst that could happen. I don't know
what survival means, if breathing is enough.
When you lose what you love, you learn to love
the loss, to guard its ache. I've tried to die
by accident—I cross the street with my eyes closed,
build fires too big for the hearth, eat casseroles
I'm sure have turned.

Every fifteen minutes,
someone shines a flashlight on my husband's chest
to check for breath. In court, he said our sons
run through the walls of his cell, curl up beside him
on his cot. When I look for them, I see
their matching headstones, my grass-stained knees.

Invitation to an Imaginary Ghost

After Donald Justice

Tonight, the radio determined to play
our every song, I hear your voice

in static crack and hiss. The porch bulb dims,
surrenders, dark. At fifteen, I didn't know

how to move my body toward yours.
We leaned against your deer-smashed grille,

the cab cluttered with sheet music and ash.
Afterward, only rumors: Austin or Denver;

needle in your arm, guitar in its case;
university or prison. You prepared each day

to meet your death. Your shackled eyes
read sorrow every time it failed to find you.

In the years I've lost since last we met,
I've cut the braids I wore to please you.

The ink on your ankles and shoulder fades
as fast as dreams I want to keep. If my words

call you to my door, I'll know what to say
when it opens. My best, first ghost,

for all my love and careful questions,
I'll never know if you're alive.

Reunion

After a week, the police thought I was dead.
He kept me three years. *The basement years*,
I called them when I had friends again,
and they'd laugh, thinking of themselves
from seventeen to twenty, the difference
that time makes.

There won't be a reunion
where the cops apologize and my parents swear
they never stopped believing. Ten years
was barely long enough for me to believe
I was free, but too long for time to stand still.
My mother died of breast cancer, my father from—
no one will say *a broken heart*, but I know
that's what they mean. I wonder if my parents
were disappointed not to find me waiting
when they died, or if they'd missed me so long
it didn't matter.

People look through me,
as though the snapshots on the news, sweater
logged into evidence, mean more than the life
I've made. I would have come back sooner
if I could, but I had to be sure I'd survived.

A Year and a Day

Someone told me it takes a year and a day
to know our dead aren't working late,
on vacation without us, asleep in the next room,

that we need to see each season change,
need to celebrate—or ignore—Thanksgiving,
Easter, our birthdays and anniversaries—

before we stop waiting for them to come home
with souvenirs, a briefcase. *An old wives' tale*,
I thought. Each night I slept beside his ghost.

Each day I poured his coffee, put away
his books, walked through space he used to fill.
On the second day of the second year

since his death, I woke without his bones
grinding my skin, his slow machinery of breath.
A year and a day: how long I had to live

with death to know I was still alive.

The Ghosts I Want

If we make our dead the way we make
our lives, I choose *ghosts in case*
of emergency. I know their stories:
the racecar driver who swears his dead
father's hands closed around his ribcage
and pulled him from a flaming crash;
miners who escaped a cave-in
by following the lamp of a co-worker
they'd never met; a woman whose life
was saved by a housecall from a doctor
dead six weeks. How much better
than guardian angels, these ghosts who love
the living too much to let them die?

Each event ends with evidence
of impossibility: video reveals
the son's body jerking backward,
nearly falling, as he untangles
burning legs from the steering wheel.
When rescue workers reach him,
he's standing feet from the flames.
The miners gather on the surface,
every man accounted for except
their savior John, whose death by cave-in
is commemorated on a plaque
outside the shaft. Fully recovered, the woman
finds the doctor's daughter emptying
his apartment of everything except
his leather bag, unused for years.

These are the ghosts I want, those able
to save me from illness or occupational
hazard. Thus far I've relied on hauntings
by the yet-undead. Driving an ice-
stormed interstate, I imagine my father
in the passenger seat: *Nice and steady,*
now tap your brake, good girl.
Examining a friend's minor injury,
I echo my mother's voice: *It's just*
a sprain. Get some ice and you'll be fine.

Given the demanding schedules
of the dead, I'm saving my haunting
for a *real* emergency. I need to know
that when the elevator falls or stairwell
fills with smoke, when my car overturns
or body derails, when the living fail me
for the last time, an appropriate ghost
is waiting to be my last resort.

Acknowledgments

Grateful acknowledgment is made to the publications in which some of the poems in this book first appeared (sometimes in slightly different form):

ABZ: "Housekeeping," "Invitation to an Imaginary Ghost," and "Overtime"

The American Poetry Journal: "Sarah Winchester Speaks"

Barrow Street: "Inventory"

Connecticut Review: "Living Without the Dead"

Crab Orchard Review: "The Ghosts I Want"

FlatCity Press Anthology 2005: "Commemoration"

Harpur Palate: "The Amateur Resurrectionist"

La Fovea: "Hank Williams, holy Father" and "The Unseen Ghosts"

The Los Angeles Review: "Spirit Winter"

Poet Lore: "The Logic of Grief"

Additionally, some of these poems appeared in the chapbook *Ghost-Writing* (Pudding House, 2007).

About the Author

Carrie Shipers received a Bachelor of Arts degree and a Master of Arts in English from the University of Missouri-Columbia and a Master of Fine Arts in Creative Writing from Ohio State University. In 2010, she completed a Ph.D. in English at the University of Nebraska-Lincoln. Her poems and reviews have appeared in a number of literary journals, including *Connecticut Review*, *Crab Orchard Review*, *Hayden's Ferry Review*, *North American Review*, and *Prairie Schooner*. She is the author of two chapbooks, *Ghost-Writing* (Pudding House, 2007), and *Rescue Conditions* (Slipstream, 2008).

I thank the University of Nebraska-Lincoln and the Nebraska Summer Writers' Conference for their support.

Thank you to Andrea Scarpino, my best, first reader. Thank you to Hilda Raz for her mentorship and support, to Ted Kooser for his feedback on these poems, and to Dorianne Laux for helping me shape the collection. Special thanks to John McKernan and Mark Halliday for seeing the book inside the manuscript.

Thank you to my parents and to my husband, Randal, who make everything possible.

LaVergne, TN USA
05 April 2010
178179LV00002B/1/P

9 780980 156027